The
Shirley
Muldowney
Story

Kieran McGovern

First published 1996 by
Phoenix ELT
Campus 400, Spring Way
Maylands Avenue, Hemel Hempstead
Hertfordshire, HP2 7EZ
A division of Prentice Hall International

Typeset in 10$^{1}/_{2}$/12$^{1}/_{2}$pt Times
by Heronwood Press

Printed in Heanor, England, by Heanor Gate Printing Ltd.

A catalogue record for this book is available from
the British Library.

ISBN 0-13-407909-4

5 4 3 2 1
99 98 97 96

Acknowledgements
The author and publishers wish to acknowledge, with thanks, the following photographic sources:

Barnaby's (p. 19); Ronald Grant (pp. 16, 23, 25, 51, 53); Topham
Picturepoint (p. 34).

The cover photograph is courtesy of Ronald Grant and shows Bonnie
Bedelia as Shirley Muldowney in the 1984 film *Heart Like A Wheel*.

Contents

Titles in this series:

Introduction

This story takes place in the world of drag- or hot-rod racing. In drag-racing two cars race over a very short distance. Sometimes these races are on ordinary streets. But the best hot-rod drivers race at special hot-rod race meetings.

Drag racers always start as ordinary cars. They are then changed or customised into racing cars. They are given special names and painted strange colours.

The best hot-rod racing happens in the USA. Today there are both men and women hot-rod racers. But thirty-five years ago women were not allowed to compete at official hot-rod race meetings.

One woman changed the world of drag racing. Her name was Shirley Muldowney.

Chapter 1

The late 1950s were an exciting time to be young in the USA. For the first time in history, American teenagers had their own heroes and their own money. They could buy the records of Elvis Presley, and watch the films of James Dean. And they could race cars.

On an empty road, on the edge of a small town near New York, a crowd of young people were standing around a very special car. The words MIKE THE MAGNIFICENT were painted in huge letters on the side. Mike himself was sitting on the bonnet, laughing at the crowd.

'This is the fastest car in town,' he said, 'and I'm the best driver. Nobody can beat me. Come on, who's stupid enough to want to race me?'

Most of the crowd agreed that Mike was the best driver in town. Only a short sixteen-year-old girl thought differently. Her name was Shirley Muldowney and she had loved racing cars all her life.

Shirley turned to her boyfriend. 'Jack, you can beat him,' she whispered. 'The car you built is faster than his.'

Jack shook his head slowly.

'The car can do it,' he said. 'But I don't think I can. He's already beaten me once. I can't take the pressure in these big races.'

Meanwhile Mike was taking out his wallet. 'Who wants to race me for fifty dollars?' he said taking the notes out and holding them up.

Shirley looked again at Jack. Her eyes shone with excitement. 'Race him!' she whispered. 'I know you can win.'

'Shirley, I won't race him. I don't want to look a fool in front of all these people.'

'Fifty dollars,' Mike was still shouting. 'Fifty dollars for anyone who can beat Mike the Magnificent! Is there any fool who wants to race me?'

For a few seconds there was silence. A few people looked at Jack, but he stared down at the ground. Then something extraordinary happened.

Shirley stepped forward. 'I'll race you, Mike,' she said calmly.

Everyone turned and stared at Shirley.

'You're crazy!' whispered Jack furiously.

Mike looked down at Shirley and started to laugh. 'You? But you're a girl!' He turned to the crowd. 'A woman racing driver! What next? Men on the moon?'

All the crowd was laughing now, except Shirley and Jack.

'Jack, you can't beat me,' said Mike, 'and your girl-friend certainly can't either. Tell her to go home and wash some dishes.'

There was more laughter. Jack took a long look at Shirley.

'I can do it, Jack,' she whispered. 'But I need fifty dollars.'

Jack looked across at Mike and then back at Shirley. After a long pause, he reached into his pocket and pulled out his wallet.

'Let's make it one hundred dollars,' he said, looking Mike straight in the eye.

□ □ □

The race was about to start and Shirley was sitting at the wheel of Jack's car. Ahead of her was an empty road, lit up by the headlights of some of the other cars. Approximately a quarter of a mile away was a piece of ribbon, stretched across the road. This was the winning line.

Across in the other car, Mike was making stupid faces and hanging out of the window. 'Give up, little girl!' he shouted. 'You're going to lose! You haven't a chance!'

This is what they all thought. Even Jack did not really believe that she was going to win. And he needed that hundred dollars for the new engine he wanted so much.

A boy carrying a red flag moved in front of the two cars. This was the sign for the two drivers to get ready. Shirley's hands were shaking, but she turned the key in the ignition.

'You're going to lose!' Mike was still shouting. 'Get out and walk away now. Before it's too late.'

Ignoring him, Shirley concentrated on the flag which was just thirty metres in front of the cars. Waiting for the signal to go forward was the most difficult part of the whole race. Because the race was so short it was very important to get a fast start.

At last, the boy dropped the flag and dived out of the way. Suddenly, Shirley was free, and the car was powering forward.

The cars raced alongside each other. Mike kept glancing across and shouting things which Shirley could not hear. Her attention was totally focused on the road ahead.

After a few seconds, Mike's confident grin disappeared. He looked nervous now and there was sweat on his face. Shirley was still right alongside him.

Mike moved into top gear. For a moment he was ahead.

'You've gone too early,' thought Shirley, almost not believing what was happening. 'I'm going to win!'

A moment later Shirley was changing into top gear. She powered past Mike and across the winning line. The race was over.

The cars slowed down and eventually stopped. Shirley was too tired to move. In her mirror, she could see people running down the road to join them. Mike climbed from his car. He looked very upset.

'You were lucky this time,' he shouted, but nobody believed him. He did not really believe it himself.

Jack was holding Shirley now.

'You were fantastic, Shirley,' said Jack. 'You drove a great race!'

Smiling, Shirley called out to Mike, 'Race me again next week and I'll show you I wasn't lucky.'

'You want to do this again?' said Jack. He looked surprised and not entirely happy.

'I never want to stop doing this,' said Shirley.

Chapter 2

'I want to marry your daughter, sir,' said Jack Muldowney in a loud voice. He was standing with Shirley in the kitchen of her father's house. Her father was playing cards with his friends.

The room went silent. Shirley's father dropped his cards. The other players coughed with embarrassment.

'I want to speak to you, young lady,' he said.

Jack stepped forward. 'Sir, I think. . .'

'Wait here, young man. I want to speak to my daughter alone.'

Shirley and her father went into the lounge. 'You're crazy to think of marrying so young!' he said. 'You're only sixteen and you're still at school. You need to study now. You have the rest of your life to get married.'

'But I love Jack! And he loves me.'

'Love doesn't pay the bills.'

'Jack's got a good job. He works in a garage. Everyone says that he's a great car mechanic.'

'I have nothing against Jack. He's a fine young man. But I want you to finish high school, Shirley. It's important to me. Then you can marry Jack.'

Shirley happily agreed. She loved her father and wanted to please him. And she knew that he was right about school. It was important for her to do her examinations.

They returned to the kitchen and told Jack the news.

'Thank you, sir,' he said, shaking his future father-in-law by the hand. 'I promise to look after your daughter.'

Laughing, Shirley's father said, 'I think that Shirley knows how to look after herself.'

□ □ □

Shirley kept her promise. She finished high school, and passed her examinations. A few months later she married Jack Muldowney. A baby soon arrived. They named him John.

The young Muldowney family had little money. Jack was a brilliant mechanic, but he earned a small salary. And now there were so many things to pay for! There was food and rent and clothes for little John. Shirley loved her husband and son very much. At first, she was happy to be just a wife and mother. But her passion for motor racing was stronger than ever. She knew that she was a very talented driver. Everyone agreed that she was the best 'road racer' in the area. But was she good enough to race against the professionals?

'What's the matter, Shirley?' Jack asked one evening,

Shirley put his dinner down in front of him and sighed. 'Oh, I don't know,' she said.

'Come on, tell me what's wrong. Do you miss racing cars?'

'Yeah, I miss the racing,' she said slowly. 'I can't explain what it means to me… . When I'm racing I feel like … like I'm really alive!' She walked over and kissed Jack on the cheek. 'You know how much I love you and John. I'll do anything to make you happy. But I need to race, Jack.'

Jack held out his hands to his wife. 'But you've beaten all the road racers,' he said.

Shaking her head, Shirley said, 'I need more of a challenge. Jack, I want to try and race professionally. I want to enter an official meeting and race on a proper track.'

Jack looked at his wife in amazement. 'Honey, you need a special customised car for that. It's not like racing the guys around here.'

'I can try and buy one.'

'It isn't that easy, Shirley. Remember, you're a woman... .'

'Jack... .'

'I know, honey. You're an amazing driver. I've seen you race. But the fact is that there are no registered women drag racers in the NHRA.'

The NHRA (National Hot Rod Association) organised hot-rod races. Jack explained that all professional drivers needed to register with the NHRA. Only registered drivers could compete in major competitions. No car company would sponsor a driver who was not registered. Without a car, Shirley could not enter races, and without entering races she could not get a car.

'It's impossible, Shirley.'

'Nothing's impossible,' said Shirley, and over the next few weeks she went to all the major car companies. Only Chrysler said they would sell her the car she needed. And they wanted five thousand dollars.

'Five thousand dollars?' said Jack, when Shirley told him the news. 'That's crazy. We could buy a hotel if we had that money. And still have change. We haven't even got five *hundred* dollars.'

'I know, Jack,' said Shirley quietly. 'But I'll have to get the money from somewhere.'

Jack looked at Shirley and shook his head in amazement. He was tired after a long day's work. His brain told him that the whole idea of Shirley becoming a registered driver was crazy. And yet a crazy idea of his own was forming in his mind. 'There may be another way of getting the car you need,' he said finally.

'How?'

'I think I can build one for you. It'll take me a few months, but... .'

Shirley was already throwing her arms around him. 'Oh, Jack, you can do it! I know you can.'

Chapter 3

'I'm sorry, young lady,' said the race official, 'but you can't race that car at this meeting.'

Shirley and Jack looked at each other. They were standing just a few yards from the race-track. In less than two hours the race they had been working towards for months was about to begin.

'But we've driven more than two hundred miles to enter this race,' said Shirley. 'And this car is as fast as anything here.'

The race official shrugged. 'You haven't the experience for a big race like this. This is for serious drivers.'

Shirley felt very angry. How could she get the experience if they did not let her race? 'The real reason you don't want me to race is because I'm a woman.'

The race official laughed and walked away. Shirley wanted to follow him but Jack held her back.

'He's not going to let you race, Shirley.'

Shirley looked at her husband in surprise. 'I haven't come all this way just to watch, Jack. I'm going to race.'

'But what can we do?' asked Jack.

Suddenly a voice interrupted them.

'Hey, don't give up!'

Jack and Shirley turned round to see that another driver was listening to their conversation. He was wearing white overalls with his name in big letters on the back: CONNIE KALITTA.

'Hi, I'm Connie,' he said, shaking them both by the hand. 'I was just listening to you talking to that idiot official. I thought I might be able to help you.'

'Help us?' said Shirley.

Connie smiled. 'Yeah, I hear you're a pretty good driver.'

'Thanks.'

Connie moved closer to the car. 'Did you really build this?' he asked Jack.

'Yeah.'

'It looks pretty good,' said Connie. 'I'd like to see how it races… . Listen, why don't you go over to the Official Enclosure.' He pointed to a large tent surrounded by a rope fence. 'That's where the people in charge of the race will be.'

Shirley pushed her way across to the enclosure. Inside, some fat men in suits were standing beside tables covered in food and drink.

A security guard stopped Shirley at the entrance. 'Can I see your Official Pass, please?' he asked.

'I need to speak to the organisers,' said Shirley. 'I want to enter the race.'

The security guard put up his arm to stop her going through. 'Only people with Official Passes are allowed in here. You'll have to write to the… .'

'I must see the person in charge of this race meeting!' Shirley was shouting now. Inside the tent, the people beside the food tables were looking across at her.

The security guard was very embarrassed. 'Alright,' he said, 'I'll see if I can find someone who'll talk to you.'

A few moments later the security guard returned. With him was a red-faced man who was still wiping his mouth with his napkin.

'Can I help you, lady?'

'I want to race this afternoon.'

The red-faced man stared at Shirley in amazement. Then he began to laugh. 'Is this a joke?'

Shirley stared straight into his eyes. 'I've never been more serious in my life,' she said quietly. 'And what's the problem? Is there some rule against women drivers? Are you afraid we might beat all the men?'

The red-faced man laughed again, shaking his head. 'There's no rule against women racing,' he said, 'but you need to get three other drivers to sponsor you.'

Still laughing, he took an application form from his pocket. He handed it to Shirley. 'If you can find three sponsors, you can race.'

Shirley rushed away. Behind her she could hear laughter from inside the tent.

'Do you think she'll get enough sponsors to race?' someone asked the red-faced man when Shirley had gone.

'Of course not!' he replied. 'Who's going to sponsor a woman racing driver? Women were made to be in the kitchen, not in racing cars. Waiter, more champagne, please!'

Chapter 4

Shirley walked over to the pits, the place where the mechanics prepare the cars that are going to race. Smoke from the engines burnt her throat, and petrol fumes mixed with the smells of hamburgers and hot dogs.

The drivers moved around the pits nervously. They were all concentrating on the race to come, worrying about their engines and their tyres. They had no time for a young woman waving an application form in front of them.

'Excuse me,' Shirley shouted over the noise of the engines. 'I'm looking for three drivers to sponsor me for the race.'

'Sorry, lady. I've got work to do.'

'Please, sir, I wonder if you would sponsor me for the race. I'm an experienced street racer and I've won more than ten... .'

'Come on get out of here! This is not a place for a woman!'

None of the drivers would take Shirley seriously. Deeply disappointed, Shirley walked back to where her husband was still talking to Connie Kalitta.

'What happened?' asked Jack.

'They won't talk to me because I'm a woman,' said Shirley. 'But I'm not giving up.'

'No, I can't see you ever giving up!' said Connie, laughing to himself. He reached over and took the application form from her. 'Well, here's one signature. And let's see if we can get some of my friends to help out.'

Connie returned with Shirley to the pits. He was a big man, good-looking and charming too. As they walked around, Shirley saw that the other drivers had a lot of respect for Connie. He joked with some of them, and argued with others. Ten minutes later Shirley had the three signatures she needed. One of them was from 'Big Daddy' Don Garlits, a future world champion who was already a celebrity amongst hot-rod racing fans.

The door was finally open. Shirley had officially entered her first professional race.

☐ ☐ ☐

Twenty minutes until race time.

Over the public address system, the race announcer was introducing the drivers to the crowd.

'And our next competitor is making a little bit of history, ladies and gentlemen. Today we have our very first ever lady driver, Mrs Shirley Muldowney.' The race announcer paused while the crowd cheered and whistled. 'She's driving a car designed by her husband, and we wish her the very best of luck!'

Down on the track Jack helped Shirley into the car. 'How do you feel?' he asked.

'Pretty nervous!' said Shirley.

They both laughed and Jack wiped away the sweat from his face. 'I don't think I can watch!' he said. 'I'm shaking already.'

Shirley squeezed his arm. 'Don't worry!' she said. 'I'll be fine. I think this is wonderful. I love the crowds and the excitement.'

'But aren't you scared? You've never raced anywhere

like this before. There are thousands of people watching.'

'Jack, I know how important this race is. We've spent months getting ready for it. We owe money to the banks and our families and our friends. People have told me that I'm crazy. Maybe they're right, but I don't think so. I believe in myself, Jack! I know I can do it.'

Jack did not know what to say. He loved and admired his wife. The problem was that he sometimes felt that he did not really understand her.

All official hot-rod races were exactly a quarter of a mile long. The starting flag was replaced by a special set of lights known as the 'Christmas tree'. The 'countdown' before a race involved the lights changing in a special order. The signal to race was when the 'Christmas tree' lights turned green.

Although drivers raced against each other the race was actually against the clock. On the start line was a special 'time beam'. As soon as the driver crossed 'time beam' the clock started. Another time beam along the finish line stopped the clock. The tension increased as the two drivers revved their engines. It was going to be a straight battle between two very fast cars. To start a split second early meant disqualification. To start a split-second late meant certain defeat. There could only be one winner.

Which car would be the fastest? Which driver would be the strongest?

The lights changed to green, and the cars raced forward. To the astonishment of the crowd, it was Shirley who powered ahead. The parachute brakes went up and the result was confirmed.

'This is unbelievable!' yelled the commentator. 'First-time driver Shirley Muldowney has won! And she has set a new track record!'

Chapter 5

Shirley Muldowney became a full-time professional hot-rod racer. She travelled across the east coast of the United States to race in places like New York State, Philadelphia and New Jersey. Because Jack was her mechanic, he travelled with Shirley to races. Young John came too.

Spending so much time on the road was very tiring. Sometimes the Muldowney family spent weeks away from home, staying in different hotels. Shirley and Jack began to argue more and more.

Jack Muldowney was a proud man, and he found his new life very difficult to accept. Shirley was beginning to attract some publicity. In every new town journalists were interested in the idea of a woman racing driver. And hot-rod racing fans were beginning to recognise Shirley's name.

People started talking about Jack as 'Shirley's husband'. This made feel Jack feel foolish and uncomfortable. What made things worse was that Jack was not really enjoying the work he was now doing.

Jack had always loved cars and was an excellent mechanic. But in professional car racing everyone has to be completely dedicated to winning races. And Jack always liked to work in his own way.

Mistakes were happening. Shirley's car was breaking down during races. It was not good enough and everyone

Shirley, Jack and John Muldowney (from the 1984 film
Heart Like A Wheel)

knew it. Connie saw the problems that Shirley was having and offered to help.

'No, we'll be all right,' said Shirley, again and again.

But it was a fact that Shirley needed a specialist racing mechanic if she was going to be successful. She needed someone like Connie.

□ □ □

Like Grand Prix racing, hot-rod racing is divided into different classes. The three basic classes of hot-rod racing are 'production', 'street', and 'super street'. All cars must be 'street legal' which means that they could legally be driven on ordinary roads.

In 'production' class, races are between normal cars. Only very small adjustments to the engine are allowed. This means that almost any car can qualify to race. But in 'super street', cars are customised specially for racing. Few people would ever want to drive a 'super street' car to work or to go shopping!

Drivers have to progress up the levels before they can qualify to race the fastest cars. The higher the class, the more expensive it is to build a suitable car. Only the very best drivers get the chance to drive in the top class.

The next stage for Shirley was to move up to what was known as 'funny' car racing. The 'funnies' were basically ordinary cars with extraordinary engines. They were called 'funny' because they looked so strange. Funny car engines looked too big for their cars, and each 'funny' had its own distinctive appearance. Most were painted in wild colours, and some were covered in cartoon drawings.

Crowds loved funny cars, but many drivers did not

like them at all. Many thought that 'funnies' were far too dangerous. During the 1960s, all motor sports were more dangerous than they are today. And funny cars were especially risky because they were not specifically designed for racing.

When Shirley told Jack she was going to change to funny car racing he was furious. To him they were 'circus' cars, designed simply to entertain the crowds. He also thought that they were far too dangerous.

'They are crazy cars!' he said. 'And you are crazy to want to drive them!'

Shirley was disappointed. 'You just don't understand!' she said. 'I've done everything I can in the class I am driving in. I need to move on to something different.'

Both Jack and Shirley knew that something had changed between them. They were arguing all the time, and the tension between them was increasing. Something had to change.

After another terrible argument about funny car racing, Shirley decided that she could not continue living with Jack. She packed her things into a suitcase and drove off into the night. The next day she phoned her eight-year-old son.

'Darling, Daddy and I can't live with each other any more,' she said, trying to hold back the tears. 'We love each other, but it's just no good.'

John said nothing. He did not really understand.

'In a few weeks you can come and live with me, darling.'

'But mom... .'

'Go to school and take care of yourself. I'll be back for you as soon as I can.'

'Do you promise?'

A 'funny' car

'Yes, I promise.'

John loved both his parents, but his old world was coming to an end. Jack was going to stay and work in his garage. It was the only place where he was really happy. Shirley was going to continue her career in motor racing. She hoped one day to be champion. People said it was an impossible dream. But John was going with Shirley.

Chapter 6

Over the next few years Shirley Muldowney became a respected hot-rod racing driver. It was now the late 1960s and big changes were happening in the United States. The Vietnam War was dividing society, and many young people were rejecting traditional ideas about how they should behave. A big movement was developing to demand equal rights for everyone, and to stop race and sex discrimination.

The National Hot Rod Association (NHRA) was a little suspicious of these changes. It seemed to see hot-rod racing as a 'man's world', and only allowed women to compete in the less respected production classes. Shirley struggled to change both the rules and the old ways of thinking. She forced the NHRA to understand that women drivers could compete equally with men.

For many hot-rod racing fans, the most famous women connected with the sport were the mascots. These were models who helped to promote NHRA events. They appeared in swimming costumes at race meetings, or on calendars produced by the NHRA.

All through her career Shirley struggled to be recognised as a serious professional. Yet despite her success on the track, Shirley began to be marketed in the same way as the mascots. She was photographed in short skirts, and given the nickname 'Cha-Cha'. Soon, advertisements appeared in which Shirley promoted products like perfume. Connie Kalitta, now Shirley's manager, thought her new sexy image was wonderful.

It was because of her success that people outside racing were becoming interested in Shirley. And after years of struggling to finance her racing, it was nice to earn enough money to make her life more comfortable. Yet Shirley never forgot that she was a driver, not a model.

'What's a beautiful girl like you doing at a place like this?' asked one journalist before a big race.

'Winning,' Shirley replied.

Shirley knew better than anyone that hot-rod racing was not about pretty clothes and perfume. It was tough, dirty and very dangerous. Soon, she was going to learn just how dangerous.

Both on and off the track, Shirley was now heavily involved with Connie Kalitta. As the first driver ever to go faster than 200 miles per hour, Connie was one of the best-known drivers in hot-rod racing. Connie called himself 'The Bounty Hunter'. Shirley now drove a car named 'The Bounty Huntress'.

Behind the official partnership there was now also a personal relationship. Connie and Shirley had become lovers, but this was being kept secret. John Muldowney sometimes travelled with his mother to race meetings, and Shirley did not want to upset her son. There was also the problem that Connie was a married man, who still officially lived with his wife.

In 1972 Connie and Shirley both entered for a big race meeting at Orange County International Raceway in California. This was Shirley's first race on the west coast. It was a chance for her to prove that she could compete against the best drivers in the whole of the USA.

Once again Shirley proved she could race well under

(From the 1984 film Heart Like A Wheel*)*

23

pressure. She won her qualifying races easily, and then joined the crowd watching the big race of the day. Connie was racing 'Big Daddy' Don Garlits, who was perhaps the greatest drag racer of them all. Both drivers were very popular with spectators.

Connie and Big Daddy raced forward to a tremendous cheer from the crowd. But Connie edged into the lead and seemed to be heading for victory. Then, suddenly, he lost control of the car. A wheel came loose and 'The Bounty Hunter' skidded off the track. The car crashed into a barrier, breaking up on impact.

The crowd watched in horror as the ambulances raced towards the accident. Shirley ran after them, praying that Connie was still alive. When she reached the wrecked car she saw all that remained of the cockpit was what looked like a large dustbin. She was about to scream when somehow the fire-fighters squeezed a human shape from the cockpit. It rolled onto the floor. Then a miracle happened. Connie climbed to his feet and waved his hand to show that he was okay. A huge cheer of relief went up from the crowd.

'That was quite a ride,' said Connie, laughing as he removed his helmet.

Shirley wrapped her arms around him.

'Darling!' she cried. 'For one horrible moment I thought... .'

'I'm the Harry Houdini of racing,' laughed Connie. 'No matter how bad it is, I always escape.'

They kissed passionately, not noticing that Shirley's son was coming down the track towards them.

John Muldowney now saw with his own eyes what he had suspected for some time. He turned and walked away.

Shirley with Connie Kalitta (from the 1984 film Heart Like A Wheel)

Chapter 7

Now that her affair with Connie was becoming public, Shirley felt increasingly unhappy. She felt guilty about the other people involved, especially Connie's wife, and her son John.

Many times she thought about her father. It was he who had first encouraged her love of cars when she was a little girl. Now he was dead, and she missed him very much. She badly needed his advice.

Connie had many good qualities. He was charming and very talented. He could also be very kind. Yet what future could he offer Shirley? In her heart, she did not believe that Connie would ever divorce his wife. And could Shirley be sure that Connie would stay with her? Connie had shown more than a friendly interest in other women. This made Shirley feel angry and hurt.

On the race-track the pressures were equally intense. To compete at the highest levels, a driving team needed to make constant adjustments to its racing car. It was always looking for new ways to make it go faster. To come second was to come last.

The problem was that all these changes could affect safety. A tiny mechanical fault could cause a disaster, because at 230 m.p.h. there was little chance of surviving an accident. This was especially true with the 'funny' cars.

To make Shirley's car go faster, Connie decided to try

out a new engine cooler in 'The Bounty Huntress'. The cooler was supposed to make the car go faster without overheating the engine. The newly adjusted engine was to be tested at a night race at Pamona Fairground, Orange County, California.

There was a big crowd for what promised to be a very special event. Spectators looked down on a race-track marked out by two rows of lights, like an airport runway prepared for a night flight. It looked like a scene from a science-fiction film.

Nothing seemed quite real, and it was easy to forget that real people were sitting in the cockpits of those strange cars. For Shirley it also felt very strange to race under a black sky and bright lights. She could hear the crowd in the distance, but she could not see any human faces.

While her son John gave the engine a final check over, Shirley had a chance to do some thinking. It made her very depressed. Somehow, things were just not working out She seemed to be losing control of her life. Something had to change.

The new cooler they were about to try out might help improve the performance of the car. But the truth was that Shirley did not enjoy racing funny cars. She wanted to move up to a higher category. She wanted to race against the top drivers in cars that were designed for racing.

The 'Christmas tree' turned from red to amber. Once again, Shirley felt the excitement she always felt when a race was about to start. It was that excitement that kept her going through all the bad times.

Shirley's mind was now completely focused on the 'Christmas tree'. This was the moment she loved. This was the time when she could forget all her problems.

The lights turned to green and Shirley powered forward. Within seconds she was already pulling clear of the other driver. Victory seemed certain. But something felt wrong. The engine was vibrating strangely.

It all happened in a few seconds. Before Shirley could do anything to protect herself it was too late. An enormous explosion was turning 'The Bounty Huntress' into a ball of fire.

□ □ □

John Muldowney was now seventeen, and this was his first season working for Shirley's team. Like his mother, he loved racing cars, and he had inherited his father's talent as a mechanic. From a very young age he had wanted to help his mother become the best driver in the world.

John also knew that motor racing was an extremely dangerous sport. Every time Shirley raced, she was risking her life. It was something he tried not to think about.

Tonight at Pamona Fairground John felt a little more nervous than usual. But when The Bounty Huntress powered forward, he felt tremendously proud. His mother really was a great driver. If they gave her the chance she could show the world she could beat Connie and Big Daddy and all the great drivers. She could be the greatest of them all.

Then suddenly John Muldowney's dreams turned into a real-life nightmare. He watched in horror as Shirley's car burst into flames.

'Oh no! Mom!'

As the flames climbed into the night sky John jumped into his truck and raced towards the accident. He arrived just as his mother was tumbling out of the wrecked car. Her clothes were on fire, and she was engulfed in flames.

Ambulances and fire engines arrived at the scene as screams echoed around the track. Shirley was rolling around on the ground trying to put out the flames that had engulfed her. Moments later three fire-fighters put out the blaze with fire extinguishers.

Trembling with fear, John knelt down beside his mother. He tried to see how badly she was burned, but Shirley was wearing a protective mask. In the night light John was unable to see her face clearly. All he could see was the terrified look in her eyes.

Chapter 8

Shirley was lucky to be alive and she knew it. As she lay in her hospital bed, she relived over and over again the nightmare of the accident. She had severe burns to her face and arms, her skin was still too sore to touch. But it was the pain of remembering which made her suffer the most.

Her room in the hospital was full of 'get-well' cards and flowers. Shirley was learning just how many friends and fans she had. New visitors arrived every day.

John sat by her side for as long as he could every day. When Shirley was feeling a little better, she discussed the accident with her son.

'I was stupid, darling. I took too big a risk. It nearly cost me my life.'

'But it wasn't your fault, Mom. It was the new cooler. Everyone says so.'

'We should have tested it properly.'

'We didn't have time.'

'Right. And why didn't we have time? Because all we could think of was finding a way of making the car faster. That's how it is with the funnies. You have to take too many risks to win.'

Shirley knew that it was time for some serious thinking. Should she give up racing? Could she put her son through this terrible experience again? Seeing the fear on John's face was the worst moment of all. And maybe next time she would not be so lucky.

Nobody would think badly of Shirley if she decided to stop racing. Being the first professional woman drag racer was already a tremendous achievement. Other women drivers would continue her work.

Yet despite all the logical arguments, Shirley knew in her heart that she did not want to retire. Car racing was a passion. It was a love affair which you only gave up when you had to. Yes, it was dangerous! But you knew it was dangerous when you climbed into your first car.

To help Shirley make her decision she turned to her son. 'What do you think, John?' she said, looking straight into his eyes. 'Tell me honestly. Do you want me to give up racing?'

Her son smiled and shook his head. 'You haven't showed them your best yet, Mom. But we're going to have to change the way we do things. Safety must be the most important thing from now on.'

□ □ □

A few days after the accident, Connie came to visit Shirley. He arrived at the hospital with another woman. He told Shirley that this woman was a 'friend'. While he was at the hospital he made another 'friend' with one of the nurses.

Connie often told Shirley that she was 'the number one most important thing' in his life. Unfortunately, that was what he told all his girlfriends. Yet despite everything, Shirley was still pleased to see this kind, generous and totally unreliable man. He was another driver. He could understand.

'Oh Connie, it was horrible! I thought that I was going to die.'

Connie took Shirley in his arms and whispered words of comfort. For a few minutes she could forget all the pain. Perhaps everything was going to be all right, after all.

Chapter 9

Hot-rod racing was becoming a big business. In the early days of the sport most drivers had a single mechanic. Some even did all the mechanical work on their cars themselves.

In the old days, the car, and all the accompanying equipment, was usually transported to the race meeting in a single truck. Racing was very hard work, and a very expensive hobby. Very few drivers earned enough from the sport to cover their expenses.

Now more people were becoming interested in hot-rod racing. Local radio and television were covering events. This brought sponsorship to racing events and to individual drivers. Companies would cover the costs of a race team. In return, that team would advertise the name and products of the company.

Because racing was more expensive than ever, sponsorship was very important. Every race team needed some sort of sponsor just to compete equally. The days when hot-rod racing was a hobby were over.

A few months after her accident, Shirley returned to a race meeting as a spectator. As she made her way past all the advertisements and special product presentations, she noticed how much bigger the crowds were these days.

Connie was down in the pits with his mechanics. They were trying get his car ready in time to enter the race. When Connie saw Shirley he gave her a big welcome.

Hot-rod racing was becoming big business

But things were not going well with Connie's car, and the race was less than an hour away. He was running out of time.

A radio journalist saw Shirley and called her over.

'Great to see you here today, Shirley. I know that all your fans will be delighted to see you on your feet again.'

'It's great to be here, Ted. And I'd like to thank all my fans for the support they've given me since the accident. It's been fantastic.'

'We all love you, Shirley. And we want to know about your future plans. Will you be back here as a driver?'

'I don't have any definite plans,' said Shirley, 'but I do know one thing. I'm never racing a funny car again.'

'No more racing funny cars? That's big news, Shirley. What—' Suddenly, the sound of shouting interrupted the interview. Over in the pits a big argument was developing. 'Sorry, Shirley, it looks like we've got a bit of trouble between one of the competitors and one of the officials. I can see Connie Kalitta ... and he seems pretty angry... .'

Connie Kalitta had missed the deadline for getting his car ready. This meant that he would not be allowed to race. Extremely upset by this decision, Connie ran over to the Official Enclosure and forced his way past the security guards.

Shirley rushed after him. She knew that Connie had a very bad temper. He would only get himself into more trouble. A security guard stepped forward to stop Shirley from coming into the Official Enclosure.

'I'm sorry, lady,' he said, 'Can I see your Official Pass?'

The guard did not seem to recognise Shirley. He was obviously not a hot-rod fan.

'I'm Shirley Muldowney.'

The name meant nothing to the guard. 'I still need to see your pass.'

With Connie now shouting at one of the most important officials, Shirley tried to push past the guard. He grabbed her arms, not realising that the terrible burns from her accident were still not fully healed.

Shirley screamed with pain. This sent Connie completely out of control. He ran across and punched the man holding her. Three more security guards rushed to try and restrain him. It took two more officials, and ten more minutes to finally calm Connie down.

Chapter 10

A few days later Connie was ordered to appear before the NHRA disciplinary committee. The disciplinary committee was there to deal with drivers who broke NHRA rules. Most of these rules were to do with the actual racing, but there was a special rule about behaviour that damaged the image of the NHRA.

The meeting of the disciplinary committee was held at a five-star hotel. Connie wore a suit and tie to try and make a good impression. But as soon as he walked into the room he knew that he was in trouble. He could see from the serious faces of the committee members that they were not happy with him.

The NHRA now had many things to think about. There were sponsorship deals worth hundreds of thousands of dollars. This sponsorship relied on racing being shown on television, and the television companies wanted a sport with a good image. Drivers punching race officials was definitely not good for business!

'We take this matter very seriously,' they told him. 'Fighting is totally unacceptable, especially from one of our most senior drivers. Mr Kalitta, you are respected throughout the hot-rod racing world for what you have done on the race-track. Youngsters look to you to set an example to them. Sadly, this is not the first time that you have appeared before us accused of damaging the reputation of the NHRA.

'To set an example, we are forced to take a very severe step. We are suspending you indefinitely, and taking away your racing licence. We shall review the situation next year.'

□ □ □

Connie left the meeting feeling very angry and upset. The punishment was far worse than he had expected. He did not know if the NHRA would ever allow him to race again.

'They're killing the sport I love,' he told Shirley. 'When I first started racing a guy could fight, or get drunk, or do what he liked. Nobody cared. Now all they are interested in is television and making us look pretty.'

'Perhaps I should wear a skirt and high-heeled shoes when I'm driving?'

'I'm sure that's what they'd want.'

They both laughed. Then Shirley became serious.

'Connie, I don't want to race funnies any more.'

'You want to retire?'

'No. I want to race 'top fuel'.'

'Top fuel? But the best drivers in the world race top fuel!'

'That's right,' said Shirley. 'And I'm going to beat them. I'm going to be the number one driver in the world.'

Connie took a deep breath. 'Shirley, you know that I think you're a great driver. I haven't seen anyone better, and I've seen some pretty good ones. But where are you going to get the car to drive top fuel?'

Smiling, Shirley put her hand on his shoulder.

'You can build it for me.'

'WHAT!'

'I want you to be my crew chief.'

Connie shook his head in disbelief. Shirley watched him calmly.

'Shirley, you are one crazy lady!'

'No, I'm not,' said Shirley. 'I know I can compete with the best drivers. I just need a car.'

'And you expect me to build it?'

'Connie, you won't be able to race for at least a year. What have you got to lose?'

'I just... .'

'And this will be a chance to make things work between us. We can beat the world together. You and me.'

Connie thought for a few moments. It would be such a difficult thing to do. There would be so many problems to overcome. And yet there was something that made him believe that it might just be possible. Shirley had so much confidence in herself. Like a true champion, she believed that she was good enough to beat anyone. Could she make the impossible happen?

'I like the idea,' said Connie slowly, 'but there is a big problem.'

'What?'

'Well, I believe that you've got the ability to beat anyone on the race track. But this is not just about driving. I mean, you're a woman... .'

Shirley looked at Connie and laughed.

'I've been a woman a long time, Connie. I can live with that.'

'But I know those guys who race top fuel,' said Connie. 'And they're very old-fashioned. I don't think they'll take a woman seriously.'

'What's new?' said Shirley, shrugging her shoulders. 'The kids back home didn't think I could beat them. The

NHRA wouldn't allow me to race until I forced them to. But they'll have to take me seriously when I'm champion, won't they?'

Chapter 11

The Muldowney-Kalitta team used the 1974 season to work on the new car. Producing a racing machine good enough to compete at the top level was a tremendously expensive and difficult business. They had to pay attention to every little mechanical detail. Daily testing was needed to identify and solve technical problems. Everything had to be right.

At times it felt like they were never going to make it. When the engine kept overheating and nobody could understand why. Or when the car kept pulling to the left despite a hundred adjustments to the steering. After a fifteen-hour day when nothing seemed to go right, it was tempting just to walk away. But somehow they kept going.

Eventually, all the months of hard work produced the result they wanted. The car was ready to compete in 'top fuel' events. Despite a few minor technical problems, the car performed very well in its early races. The general impression in the hot-rod racing world was that the Muldowney-Kalitta team was going to be a serious competitor.

'The car seems to have what it takes,' said one radio journalist in an interview after an early race. 'But what about you, Shirley? Do you now think you can compete with the 'big boys'?'

'I've always thought that I could compete with anyone,' said Shirley.

But some critics continued to suggest that Shirley was not good enough to race at the top level. As at every other stage in her career, she answered them on the race-track. In 1975, Shirley Muldowney broke into the NHRA's list of the top fifteen drivers. This was a fantastic achievement, and there was better to come. In 1976, Shirley became the first woman ever to win an NHRA national event.

At last Shirley was beginning to be recognised as one of the top competitors in hot-rod racing. Her success attracted a lot of media coverage, especially when she beat 'Big Daddy' Don Garlits. Garlits was one of the greatest hot-rod drivers of all time, and he was also one of Shirley's original sponsors. It was the kind of story that radio and television companies loved.

Shirley was becoming a minor celebrity. She gave good interviews, and helped to promote hot-rod racing as much as she could.

It was nice to receive so much attention, and Shirley enjoyed appearing in public. Sometimes, however, Shirley wondered how much of this media interest was for what she did on the race-track. Everyone concentrated on the fact that Shirley was an attractive young woman. Many interviewers paid more attention to her physical appearance than to her driving.

Another thing that was beginning to annoy Shirley was the nickname 'Cha-Cha'.

'Cha-Cha, how does it feel to be the prettiest girl in hot-rod racing?' asked one chat-show host.

'Actually, Bob, my name is Shirley. 'Cha-Cha was a name that was used to promote me when I first started driving professionally. I've never liked it. And I don't know anything about being a pretty girl. I do know that I'm a very good driver.'

'I'm sure you are, Cha-Cha. But you are a lady and the other drivers are all men. Do the other guys give you special treatment?'

'I don't understand the question, Bob. What sort of 'special treatment'? Do you think the other drivers let me go in front of them?'

The interviewer laughed and winked at the audience. 'No, what I was saying, Cha-Cha—'

'Oh, I understand now! That's why I win. Because I'm a woman the other drivers let me go first.'

The studio audience clapped and cheered. But Shirley knew that people would continue to say silly things about her being a woman. The only way she could really make people take her seriously was by winning races.

In 1977 Shirley became a serious challenger for the NHRA Championship. She won three NHRA events in succession and moved to the top of the points table. She was now favourite to win the championship. Could she take the pressure?

Shirley had a reputation for being a fast starter in races. She would take an early lead and then hold on to it until the finish. And that was exactly how she won the 1977 NHRA Championship.

On the day of her championship-winning victory, Shirley was interviewed on national television by a sports journalist. He asked her what seemed a simple question.

'Shirley Muldowney, you have achieved what nobody thought was possible. You became the first professional woman hot-rod driver. Now you have won the highest prize in the sport. Where do you and Connie go from here?'

'I really don't know, Ted,' said Shirley, turning away.

It was an honest answer because behind all the smiles and celebrations there was another, very different, story. What the television journalist did not realise was that the Kalitta-Muldowney fairy-tale was heading for a very unhappy ending.

Chapter 12

'Hello, are you Shirley?'

Shirley did not recognise the voice of the woman on the phone. It sounded strange, almost angry.

'Yes, I'm Shirley. Who is this?'

'I want to speak to you. About Connie.'

Something about the way the woman spoke made Shirley feel nervous. It was the night before the race which could win her the championship. She was sharing a hotel room with Connie. He was shaving in the bath-room. They were about to go out to dinner.

'Who are you?' repeated Shirley.

'Come to the hotel coffee shop. I'll be waiting for you.'

The woman put down the phone. Shirley stared into space for a few moments. She knew that she would have to go and meet this mystery woman. She also guessed that she was not going to like what she was going to hear.

Shirley took a mirror from her bag and began brushing her hair. She could see from her face how worried she felt. This meeting was going to be worse than any race.

When Shirley arrived in the coffee shop, she saw a woman sitting alone by the door. Shirley guessed that it was the woman who had phoned from the way she was nervously smoking a cigarette. And her face seemed strangely familiar.

The woman seemed to recognise Shirley. She pointed

to the chair opposite her. 'Take a seat, Shirley. I've got something to tell you.'

Shirley sat down without saying anything.

'I'm sorry to have to tell you this, Shirley,' said the woman quickly, 'but Connie and I have a very special relationship.'

Shirley reached down and took a cigarette from her bag. She saw that her hand was shaking.

'How long has this been going on?'

'Three years,' said the woman. 'Connie and I met in Orange County Hospital.'

Suddenly Shirley remembered.

'So that's where I've seen you before. You were a nurse at the hospital I went to after my accident!'

The woman nodded.

'I'm sorry about all this, Shirley,' said the woman. 'But you must understand that Connie needs me.'

Shirley closed her eyes for a moment. Then she shook her head slowly. 'Connie wants to have us all. He wants me and you and every other girl that will have him. We're both fools to think anything else.'

Shirley got up and walked out of the coffee shop. As she passed through the lobby, Connie came out of the lift. When he saw the woman in the coffee shop he put his head in his hands. Then he followed Shirley out to her car.

'She means nothing to me,' he protested. 'She just keeps following me. I didn't want to be unkind to her. But now it's over.'

Shirley opened the door of her car and got into the driving seat.

'Shirley, you know you are the number one most important thing in my life.'

Shutting the door behind her, Shirley started the car and drove away.

□ □ □

At the awards ceremony for the 1977 NHRA Top Fuel Championship Shirley thanked all the people who had made her success possible. She thanked her son John, and her mechanic Ron Tobler. She thanked the NHRA organisers.

'And I'd also like to thank Jack Muldowney, who built my first car, and Connie Kalitta, who built my best car. Most of all, I'd like to thank my father for believing in me.'

It was a very emotional speech. Shirley left the stage in tears, just as Connie was rising to say a few words.

'I have only one person to thank,' he said, 'and that is the woman who has made it all possible, Shirley Muldowney. I've always said that Shirley is the best driver I've ever seen.'

Listening to Connie, Shirley felt so sad that tears began to roll down her face. She knew that he meant what he said and she was very moved. But she also knew that her personal relationship with Connie was over.

Shirley still felt the pain of her break-up with Jack. It was difficult for her to face the fact that her long affair with Connie was also ending in failure.

'Has it all been worth it?' she asked herself, as the tears continued to fall.

□ □ □

Connie did not realise just how unhappy Shirley was. He knew that she was upset with him, but he thought that any trouble between them would pass with time. When

Shirley told him that she wanted to end their partnership he was astonished.

At first he didn't believe her, thinking that she was just trying to make him behave better in the future. When he saw that she really was serious, he lost his temper and became very angry.

'After all I've done for you!' he shouted. 'I made you world champion.'

'Connie, I don't want us to argue about this. It would be better for both of us if we could separate peacefully.'

But Connie was furious. 'I gave you the car that won the world championship. You'll be nothing without me!'

'That's what you think, is it?' said Shirley, who was angry herself now. 'Well, I'll show you that I can win without you.'

'You're going to regret this!' said Connie furiously. 'I'm going to build the fastest car you've ever seen.'

'And who's going to drive it?' asked Shirley.

Connie looked at Shirley for a moment. Then he turned towards the door. 'I'm going to drive it,' he said. 'And I'm going to beat you at every race-track in the country!'

Chapter 13

'I want you and Ron Tobler to lead my crew team,' Shirley told her son, John. 'But it's not going to be easy.'

'I know that, Mom,' said John. 'But we can do it. I know we can.'

John Muldowney felt very proud to be one of the leaders of Shirley's team. But he knew that he was very young to be in this position. He still had a lot to learn.

Many people in the hot-rod racing world thought that Shirley was finished as a major competitor. Sponsors believed that Connie Kalitta was the main reason for her success and they now withdrew their support. This meant that Shirley had very little money. Her crew team also had very little experience of racing at the top level. Few believed that Shirley Muldowney would ever seriously compete for the championship again.

In the season following her break-up with Connie it looked as if Shirley's critics were right. She did not defend her championship successfully. In fact, Shirley did not win any major races at all.

'What's gone wrong, Shirley?' the interviewers asked. 'Can your team survive without Connie?'

'We're having a few technical problems,' replied Shirley, 'but we'll be back next year. Connie was a great crew chief, but John and Ron will be even better.'

But it was difficult for the new Shirley Muldowney team that season. Everyone who works in racing wants to win. And when things are not going well people begin to doubt themselves. John Muldowney in particular often wondered if he was good enough to be crew chief.

What kept them going was Shirley's belief in the people that worked for her. Working for the Muldowney team was not the kind of job you could just walk away from at five o'clock every evening. The hours were long and the work was hard. But Shirley made everyone understand that they were all important members of the team. And she made them believe that one day soon they would start winning again.

During the 1979 season Shirley began to improve rapidly. Many of the technical problems were solved and she won eleven races. Sponsors continued to stay away, but people who understood hot-rod racing began to take the new Muldowney team more seriously.

□ □ □

From the start of 1980 it was clear that Shirley was back to her best form. She won the Winter, Spring and Autumn meetings of the NHRA Championship to complete a sensational comeback. Once again, Shirley Muldowney had the perfect answer for those foolish enough to doubt her ability.

By the final round Shirley needed only one more victory to retake the World Championship. Only one man could stop her from being champion. By an amazing coincidence the deciding race would be against 'The Bounty Hunter', Connie Kalitta.

It was Connie's first appearance in the final round for many years. He was one of the most famous names in the the sport, but his days as a top driver seemed to be behind him.

Shirley was the clear favourite to win the race. But someone like Connie was always a difficult opponent. He believed he could beat Shirley, and he knew her driving better than most.

It was more than two years since the break-up between Connie and Shirley. Unfortunately, there was still some bad feeling between them. They had not spoken to each other since the day of the big argument. And each had read silly things that the other was supposed to have said in magazine interviews.

Now, there was some tension between the two crews before the race.

'We're going to beat you so badly you'll never race again!' they called to each other.

'Go home now before we embarrass you in front of all these people.'

It was just like the early days when Mike the Magnificent stood on his car and said: 'Which one of you

(From the 1984 film Heart Like A Wheel)

51

fools thinks he can beat me?' The first battle of any race was always in the mind.

The two cars moved to the starting line. The crowd cheered. Everyone was excited about what people were calling 'The Race of the Year'.

Shirley and Connie were now just a few feet from each other. Connie looked across and laughed. Just like Mike the Magnificent had once laughed.

Finally the lights turned green. The two cars flew off the line. Both started well and for a hundred metres they were side by side. Then Shirley began to pull away.

A tremendous race ended with Shirley crossing the finishing line first. As the parachutes went up, the cheers of the crowd could be heard for miles. The championship was Shirley's for the second time.

After the race, Shirley ran over to Connie. They embraced each other.

'That was some race,' said Shirley.

Connie smiled. 'I'll beat you next season,' he said.

□ □ □

In 1982 Shirley Muldowney became the first ever driver to win a third NHRA Top Fuel Championship. Along with Don Garlits and Jerry Ruth, she was one of only three drivers to go faster than 250 m.p.h. in a piston-engine car. In fact, she recorded four of the seven officially recorded speeds of over 250 m.p.h. Her fastest speed of 255.58 was only 0.5 seconds slower than the world record set by Jerry Ruth at Englishtown, New Jersey in July 1977.

The girl they had tried to stop racing had beaten them all. Nobody could now deny that Shirley Muldowney was one of the greatest drivers of all time.

*The 'real' Shirley Muldowney (on the left) with Bonnie Bedelia,
who played her in the 1984 film* Heart Like A Wheel

Exercises

1 Why does Jack not want to race Mike?
   a) Because he likes Mike.
   b) Because he does not think he can win.
   c) Because he wants Shirley to race Mike.

2 Why does Jack think that it will be 'impossible' for
   Shirley to race in an official meeting?
   a) Because he does not think Shirley is good enough.
   b) Because the NHRA does not allow women to drive.
   c) Because Shirley will not be able to get a customised
      car.

3 What does Shirley need to register for the race?
   a) A new car.
   b) Three sponsors.
   c) To change into a man.

4 What happens in Shirley's first official race?

5 Why does Jack not want Shirley to drive 'funny' cars?

6 What happened to Connie at the Orange County
   International Raceway?

7 What happened at Pamona Fairground?

8 What do John and Shirley decide after Shirley's
   accident?

9 Why did Connie punch the race official?

10 Why does Shirley think that Connie should be her crew chief?

11 What does Shirley think about people calling her 'Cha-Cha'?

12 In what year did Shirley first win the NHRA Championship?

13 What do people think when the Muldowney-Kalitta team breaks up?

14 What were the problems that the new Muldowney team had?

15 How many times did Shirley win the World Championship?
   a) Once.
   b) Twice.
   c) Three times.

Glossary

3   **gear** (n): system in cars and bicycles for changing speed
'Mike moved into top gear.'

7   **hot-rod** (adj): a car that has been customised (see above) for racing
'The NHRA organised hot-rod races.'

37   **impression** (n): the effect of something or somebody on a person
'… to try and make a good impression.'

17   **legal** (adj): allowed by law
'All cars must be 'street legal'…'

5   **mechanic** (n): someone who works with machines
''Everyone says that he's a great car mechanic.''

7   **registered** (v): to be on an official list
''…there are no registered women drag racers.''

24   **spectator** (n): to be part of a crowd watching something
'Both drivers were very popular with spectators.'

7   **sponsor** (v): to help and support a person or a team, often by giving money
'No car company would sponsor a driver who was not registered.'

21   **struggled** (v): to fight for something that is difficult to get
'… Shirley struggled to change both the rules and the old ways of thinking.'

28   **vibrating**   to shake powerfully
'The engine was vibrating strangely.'

Language Grading in the Phoenix ELT *Bookshelf* Series

This reader has been written using a loosely controlled range of language structures. There is no tight control of vocabulary as it is based on the authors' experience of the kind of vocabulary range expected at each particular language level. The authors have also taken care to contextualise any unfamiliar words, which are further explained in the glossary. We hope you will try to deduce meaning from the context, and will use a dictionary where necessary to expand your lexical knowledge.

The language items listed here show those most commonly used at each level in the ***Bookshelf*** series:

Level One (elementary)
Mainly simple and compound sentences, beginning to use more complex sentences but with limited use of sub clauses.

Present Simple	Positive and negative statements
Present Continuous (present and future reference)	Interrogative
	Imperative
Past Continuous	And, or, but, because, before, after
'Going to' future	Some/any (-thing)
Past Simple (regular and a few common irregular)	Basic adjectives
	Some common adverbs
Can (ability)	'Simple' comparatives, superlatives
Would like (offer, request)	Gerunds/infinitives, common verbs

Level Two (lower intermediate)
Simple and compound sentences, limited use of complex sentences.

Present Perfect	Conditional, can, could (possibility)
Will/won't future	When/while
Present/Past Simple Passive	Question tags, reflexives
Have to, must, should, could	Comparatives, superlatives
Can/may (requests/permission)	(common adjectives/adverbs)
Infinitives (like, want, try, etc.)	Reported speech (present/past)
Gerunds (start, finish, after, like, etc)	

Level Three (intermediate)
More complex sentences, including embedded clauses.

Present Perfect Continuous	May/might (possibility)
Past Perfect	Conditionals 1 and 2
Present/Past Continuous Passives	Although, to/in order to, since (reason)
Perfect Passives	So/neither
Ought to	Reported statements, requests, etc.

Level Four (upper intermediate)
At this stage there is minimal control, although authors generally avoid unnecessary complexity.

Future Continuous	More complex passives
Past Perfect Continuous	Conditionals 3